James Ramsay, James Phillips, J. S. Smith

A Letter From Capt. J.S. Smith to the Revd. Mr. Hill

On the State of the Negroe Slaves

James Ramsay, James Phillips, J. S. Smith

A Letter From Capt. J.S. Smith to the Revd. Mr. Hill
On the State of the Negroe Slaves

ISBN/EAN: 9783744687928

Printed in Europe, USA, Canada, Australia, Japan

Cover: Foto ©ninafisch / pixelio.de

More available books at **www.hansebooks.com**

A

LETTER

FROM

CAPT. J. S. SMITH

TO THE

REV^D MR HILL

ON THE

STATE

OF THE

NEGROE SLAVES.

[*Now in the Pre/s.*]

An ESSAY on the SLAVERY and COMMERCE of the HUMAN SPECIES, (but particularly the African) being the Subſtance of a Latin Diſſertation, which was honoured with the firſt Prize, in the Univerſity of Cambridge, for the Year 1785.

A

LETTER

FROM

CAPT. J. S. SMITH

TO THE

REV^D MR HILL

ON THE

STATE

OF THE

NEGROE SLAVES.

———————

To which are added

An INTRODUCTION,

AND

REMARKS ON FREE NEGROES, &c.

BY THE EDITOR.

———————

LONDON:

PRINTED and SOLD by J. PHILLIPS, in GEORGE-
YARD, LOMBARD-STREET. 1786.

INTRODUCTION.

A Neighbour of mine having sent to a gentleman of his acquaintance my Essay on the Treatment and Conversion of African Slaves in the Sugar Colonies, with a desire that he would read it attentively, and give his opinion of it impartially: that request produced the following Letter, which appeared to me to be of so much importance, and to be so decisive in the present controversy, that through my neighbour I begged the writer's permission to make it publick; to which he very obligingly gave his consent. But before I present it to the reader, it is necessary to premise a few introductory remarks.

The answers that have been given to my Essay consist of two parts, the *vindictive* and the *argumentative*. The former exhibits a long list of personal invec-

A tives,

tives, which are the groffeft infult on truth, on common juftice, and common decency, that can be imagined; and were manifeftly intended to draw off the attention of the publick from the main queftion to fubjects of private altercation, and to leffen the weight and credit of the Effay, by traducing and vilifying the writer of it. From a regard to the *caufe* therefore, no lefs than to myfelf, I thought it neceffary to clear away all this rubbifh of obloquy and falfhood. This I attempted in my *Reply*; and, in the opinion of gentlemen who are by no means partial to me, I have there completely vindicated my character from every charge that my induftrious antagonifts have, with infinite pains, collected together againft me.*

---

* " To us Mr. R. appears to have completely vin-
" dicated his own character and conduct againft every
" article of impeachment, of any material confequence,
" that hath been urged in the debate." Monthly Review, January, 1786, p. 28.

In

In doing this, it was my ferious aim, whilft I was defending my own character as a man and an author, to enter no farther into thofe of my adverfaries than they themfelves had blended them with their opinions. If, however, in attempting this, it fhall be thought by cool impartial judges, who know neither them nor me, that I might have been fomewhat lefs circumftantial, and that the keen feelings of an innocent and much injured man fhould have been kept more under the government of that Chriftian moderation, which fhews itfelf moft eminently in the fevereft trials, I bow to the reproof; and fhall only requeft the candid reader to make thofe allowances, which the uncommon fituation I was placed in may fairly claim, and which in cafes of felf-prefervation and felf-defence are never denied: for even in the judgment of their advocates, my antagonifts were the *aggreffors*.*

* Monthly Review, January, 1786.

As

As to the *argumentative part*, (if it deserves that name) it is so thinly scattered through the answers to my *Essay*, and so very feebly supported, that I might very safely have rested the whole merits of the cause on the Essay, without paying the smallest regard to the objections of my opponents. Of those objections, however, such as they are, I have in my *Reply* taken as much notice as they appeared to deserve : and there I meant to have left this controversy. But some friends have lately suggested to me, that there were two points of so much importance, as to claim a fuller consideration than I had there room or leisure to give them. These are 1st, *The general ill treatment, and present wretched condition of the negroe slaves in the British sugar colonies.* 2dly, *The possibility of cultivating the sugar cane by free hired labourers, either black or white.*

Both these positions my antagonists have denied with so much confidence and

and vehemence, and have given repre-
fentations of them fo diametrically oppofite to truth, that perfons who have
never been in the Weſt Indies, and ſeen
with their own eyes what is daily paſſing
there, may poſſibly (it is faid) be ſtag-
gered by ſuch bold aſſertions.

With reſpeƈt to the firſt of theſe,
*The general ill treatment, and preſent
wretched condition of the negroe ſlaves in
the Britiſh ſugar colonies*, did I think it
neceſſary, I might corroborate the abun-
dant proofs given in the Eſſay, by the
teſtimonies of many living witneſſes, and
by quotations from a multitude of authors of undoubted credit, whoſe repre-
fentations of the ſtate of the negroes,
each in proportion to his degree of in-
formation, are perfeƈtly confonant to
mine.* But I really did not conceive it
to

---

* Among many others that might be named, I will
only beg leave to refer the reader to theſe that follow
Raynal's Hiſtoire Politique et Philofophique, vol. iv.

A 3   p. 5, 6, 7.

to be incumbent on me to adduce such an accumulation of evidence in support of a fact too plain to be controverted. It seemed to me the same thing as going about to prove, by a long train of formal arguments, that *it was light at noon day.* The general ill treatment and misery of the negroes is a fact denied by *none,* but those who are *interested* in denying it.

p. 5, 6, 7. Benezet's Caution to Great Britain, &c. 1767. His Historical Account of Guinea, 1772. Thoughts on Slavery, by Mr. John Wesley; Hawes, 1774. Dean Tucker's Reflections on the Disputes between Great Britain and Ireland, p. viii. 17. Cadell, 1785. Account of the European Settlements in America, vol. ii. p. 120—127. Essays Historical and Moral, by G. Gregory, Essay XVII. and XVIII. Mr. Grenville Sharpe's various Tracts on Negroe Slavery. Sir H. Sloan's Voyage to Barbadoes, &c. 1707. All these gentlemen have described the cruelties exercised on the negroes in stronger colours, and treated the authors of them with more indignation and severity, than are to be found in my Essay. What then will my adversaries say to these respectable writers? Were all these influenced by motives of resentment to traduce the West India Planters? Were such men as these actuated only by *vulgar prejudices?*

A few

A few men of this defcription, it is allowed, have contradicted my affertions; or rather the affertions of all who have ever treated of the fubject. But contradiction is not confutation. And if the authenticity of the two oppofite accounts be fairly weighed againft each other, to which of the refpective authors is moft credit due? To *thofe*, who thought fit to appear in the character of anonymous pamphleteers, and who, from their connections abroad, are too much parties concerned, too much under the influence of intereft and refentment, to be impartial or competent witneffes in the caufe: or to *him*, who boldly, and in the firft inftance, fets his name to his work; who rifks his reputation on the truth of his affertions; who forms no claim; complains of no difappointment; who could not (if in his fenfes) take fo abfurd a way of gratifying his pique, or recommending himfelf to favour, as that of publifhing to the world a ftring

of

of falſhoods, which thouſands might confute the next moment; who, for near twenty years together, was an eye witneſs of the facts he relates; and who, in fine, had not, and could not poſſibly have, any other motive for expoſing him-ſelf to that clamour and obloquy, which he *foreſaw* he ſhould incur (though not in the degree he has ſince endured) from a numerous and powerful body of men, but the ſincereſt and moſt heart-felt compaſſion for thoſe wretched creatures, whoſe advocate he had been perſuaded publickly to become? Let the candid reader attentively weigh this ſtriking contraſt of circumſtances between ſuch a man and his opponents, and it is im-poſſible he can be at any loſs what opi-nion to form of their reſpective narra-tives.

But if the ſmalleſt doubt ſhould ſtill remain on his mind, it will, I appre-hend, be effectually removed by the fol-lowing

lowing letter: it is written by a gentleman, a captain in his majefty's navy,
who is a ftranger to me, who certainly
has no fpleen to gratify, and no patronage
to court; but voluntarily and generoufly
gives his teftimony from a love of truth,
and to do juftice to the writings of a
man, whom he confiders as moft inju-
rioufly and cruelly treated. This, if any
thing can be fo, is clear, impartial, fatif-
factory, decifive evidence.

T O

THE REVEREND MR. HILL,

EAST MALLING.

DEAR SIR,

I Should have acknowledged the receipt of your note, and Mr. Ramfay's Effay fooner, but fhortly after it came to hand, I was under an engagement to vifit Brumpton; and had I not been taken ill there, meant to have vifited Malling before my return home. However, I have now the pleafure to inform you I am getting better of my old complaint; and take this earlieft opportunity of doing juftice to a man, who appears to me to have been grofsly ill-treated by anonymous writers.

The

The ill treatment of flaves is too well known, and too univerfal, to be denied. I do affirm, I have feen the moft cruel treatment made ufe of at feveral of the Weft India Iflands, particularly at Antigua. While ferving on that ftation, ten years ago, I vifited feveral of the plantations there. In confequence of meeting with an old fchool-fellow, who managed an eftate on that ifland, I was introduced to many of that defcription; and too often has my heart ached to fee *the cruel punifh-ments, for trifling caufes,* inflicted by the manager with fuch unconcern, as not to break in upon his jocularity. When I have interfered, I have been afked, " Do you " not punifh on board fhips?" My anfwer was, " Yes, no doubt, but not in this " cruel way." — A poor negroe laid ftretched flat on his face on the ground, at his peril to move an inch, till the punifhment is over; that inflicted with a whip, whofe thong, at the thickeft part, was the fize of a man's thumb, and tapering

pering longer than a coachman's whip. At every ſtroke a piece was taken out by the particular jerk of the whip, which the manager (ſometimes his wife) takes care to direct. This I have often ſeen for not getting a ſufficient quantity of graſs for the manager, (for I well know more goes to his ſhare than his maſter's)* and many ſuch trifling things.

It is no uncommon thing for a negroe to lie by a week after puniſhment. *That*, I ſhould conceive, would be of no advantage to the proprietor, however neceſſary the puniſhment may be conſidered. I am truly ſorry to ſay, there are too many of the opinion of Plutarch; and I beg leave to differ very widely from them: for I have had ſome dealings with negroes, and I cannot ſay I ever found them ſo egregiouſly ſtupid as is deſcribed. I rather found them keen, ſenſible

* Note by the editor. This muſt be meant for the manager's own live ſtock, ſheep, goats, &c.

people;

people; and fhould imagine, were they treated properly, and not driven to thofe extremes, which are attributed to their vicious difpofitions, they would be as tractable as white people. Of this truth I am fatisfied, from what I have feen at the ifland of Grenada. I vifited a gentleman there, who lived about fix miles from the Carenage; and had the pleafure of obferving fuch a wonderful difference of treatment as aftonifhed me. After dinner, we were enjoying the bottle, and were fuddenly furprized by a pleafing melancholy finging. We broke up from table, and found (as I underftood was the ufual cuftom) the poor negroes juft returned from their labour, finging hymns at the door, and with fuch decency and decorum, expreffive of the moft heart-felt love for the manager, as made me exclaim againft the treatment I had feen at Antigua. The manager gave me to underftand, it was the conftant mode in that diftrict; which is called the French quarter. There

were

were no cruelties exercifed any where near *him*. In other parts of the ifland, it was the fame as in other iflands; but he had always a particular fatisfaction in returning home to his plantation, finding his negroes do much better, than thofe who are treated with fuch inhuman feverity. He acknowledged, he had occafion to punifh; but did not find it neceffary to do it often, or with that cruelty, *fo univerfal in other iflands.* We went with him to vifit the huts, which he affured us was his conftant cuftom, and afked the negroes in the different huts, if they were fatisfied, or wanted any thing. It is impoffible to defcribe my feeling on this occafion: not a fingle negroe diffatisfied, (I think the number three hundred) nor the driver any complaint to make. If this is to be accomplifhed *in one fet of negroes,* why not *in any other?* This plan the gentleman told me he found when he came to the eftate. *It originated in the French.* Moft of the

negroes

negroes fpoke French; and one very well informed amongft them kept a fchool for young negroes. This and many more inftances fully convince me, that *flaves in general are not properly treated.* They have fine feelings as well as we, and only want *cultivation.*

I perfectly agree with Mr. Ramfay in every part of his Effay, which I have read very attentively; and was I to obferve on every page, could comment more voluminoufly than I hope is neceffary: I fhall therefore only obferve a few particulars, and conclude for this time, till, on any future occafion, Mr. Ramfay may find occafion to call upon me.

It is too fhocking for an Englifhman, on his firft going to the Weft Indies, to pafs a plantation where the negroes are at work, and hear the violent ftrokes from the unmerciful whip before defcribed, for perhaps only looking at a ftranger paffing

paffing by, and not going on with the work at the fame time. *This I have feen many a time in different iflands,* and that in the heat of the day; and many poor wretches have I met on the road with backs too fhocking to defcribe. The laft act of humanity or kindnefs (as it is called) fhewn to a negroe after he is worn out by hard work, fevere punifhment, or ficknefs from unwholefome food, is to give him his freedom, *too often, when he can fcarcely crawl or fpeak.* Too many well known inftances happen of that kind in all the iflands, a treatment which furely wants attending to. It is very uncommon in England for a man to turn his worn-out horfe loofe to feek his living.

It is aftonifhing that any man will prefume to affirm that the negroes are better treated than the peafantry in England. The real fact is, that the firft fentiment entertained, by a ftranger, of a fet or gang of negroes going to work, or at work, is

B   neither

neither more nor lefs than of a drove of cattle going to Smithfield market, or cattle working under unmerciful drivers. It fhocks me much to recollect the comparifon.

I hope what I have related may prove ufeful to Mr. Ramfay. I feel for any man, who is contradicted in circumftances too well known to admit of contradiction; and he has my permiffion to ufe my name on the occafion, when and where he pleafes.

I am,

SIR, &c.

Newington,
28th Jan. 1786.

J. S. SMITH.

After

After the perufal of this letter, the reader will be inclined to think, that the facts in my *Effay* are perfectly conformable to truth; and that I am not the *only* eye-witnefs, who maintains that *the negroes are cruelly treated.* They, who have occafion to vifit the Weft Indies, need only caft their eyes on the backs of a gang of flaves at work. They will there fee but too evident and convincing proofs of the facts afferted by Captain Smith and me. But perfons who have never croffed the Atlantick, and cannot have this ocular demonftration, muft be content with the beft evidence that the nature of the thing admits; that is, with fuch evidence as is contained in the preceding letter. Captain Smith, we fee, affirms, that *the ill treatment of the negroes is too well known, and too univerfal to be denied.* Neither is it, nor the cruel hardfhip of grafs-picking, confined to St. Chriftopher; they extend to Antigua, and other iflands; even Grenada, where

the good effects of a different management might have taught mafters better,
continues to fuffer under the inhuman
influence. He affirms alfo, in conformity
to what I have advanced, and never till
now heard denied, that *the French ufe
their flaves with more lenity and gentle-
nefs than the Englifh*; and that he himfelf
faw a ftriking and moft pleafing proof of
it in Grenada.* He declares in fine, without

---

* This clear teftimony of Captain Smith is confirmed
by many other writers of credit. " The negroes in our
" colonies endure a flavery more complete, and attended
" with far worfe circumftances than what any other
" people in their condition fuffer in any other part of
" the world, or have fuffered in any other period of
" time." Account of European Settlements in America, vol. 2. p. 120.

" One thing is fo notorious, that it cannot be denied,
" viz. That the Englifh planters, *in general*," (doubtlefs
there are exceptions) " treat their flaves, or fuffer them
" to be treated, with a greater degree of inhumanity,
" than the planters of any other European nation."
Dean Tucker on the Difpute between Great Britain and
Ireland, p. 10.

" You

out referve, that *he agrees with me in every part of my Effay;* and owns that he cannot help feeling for any man, who is contradicted in circumſtances too well known to admit of contradiction.

" You carry the furvivors" (thofe who furvive the voyage from Africa) "into the vileſt flavery, never to " end but with life: fuch flavery as is not found among " the Turks at Algiers," (fee a quotation in my Reply from Baron Tott) " no nor among the Heathens in " America." Wefley's Thoughts on Slavery, p. 24. Mr. Wefley may be confidered, from his refidence in Georgia, as a competent eye-witnefs. Indeed, had I feen this little work before mine was publiſhed, I ſhould have thought myfelf obliged to have written in a more warm and decifive manner. His account of the negroe coaſt of Africa, the happy ſtate of its inhabitants, their advancement in the arts of life, the fatal effects of their intercourfe with the Europeans, the deſtructive violent nature of the flave trade; all agree with every inquiry I have been able to make. To whatever he fays of their treatment in the colonies, I add my voluntary teſtimony, as to a thing within my own obfervation. His reafoning I think full and conclufive; and am happy to find that, writing at a diſtance, and without any concert, and only drawing from one common fountain, experience, we agree in almoſt every conclufion.

B 3   The

The reader now fees with what juftice I have been accufed of aggravating the miferies of the negroes, and of calumniating and grofsly mifreprefenting Weft Indian planters. It appears, that I have advanced nothing but what is confirmed by the moft authentick teftimony, as well as by almoft every author (except my opponents) who has written on the fubject. And there are numbers of gentlemen, *now in this kingdom*, well acquainted with the Weft Indies, who have repeatedly faid to me, *in converfation*, what Captain Smith has had the generofity to fay in *print*. Indeed, among thofe who have feen our fugar colonies, *and have no property in them, nor connection with them*, there is but one opinion on this point. But every one does not choofe (and I do not much wonder at it) to commit himfelf in publick with the whole body of Weft Indian planters.

As

As to myfelf, I have a juſt eſteem for theſe gentlemen, and think them a valuable, reſpectable claſs of men. Theſe ſentiments I have voluntarily and publickly avowed in many parts of my Eſſay, and my Reply; and in both, and in my Inquiry into the African trade, have repeatedly acknowledged that many of them treat their ſlaves with humanity and kindneſs.* I ſhould be ſhocked at the

* See Eſſay, p. 76. 87. 91. and 100. See Preface to Inquiry, &c. The reader may there ſee that *I have not loaded the planters with odious private abuſe.* On the contrary, I have produced inſtances of their good management and humanity, and dwelt on them with apparent ſatisfaction. Neither is it true that *I have hung up the private characters of living individuals to publick deteſtation and abhorrence.* It was neceſſary that I ſhould confirm my aſſertions by ſome *particular facts,* otherwiſe I ſhould have been accuſed of *vague and general declamation.* But I mentioned no perſon by name; and thoſe alluded to were either no more, or happily beyond the influence of cenſure. Nay, ſo far am I from being judged guilty of having written my Eſſay with too much warmth, or acrimony, that I am cenſured by the friends of my opponents for being too cool, for not

having

the idea of giving one moment's unneceſſary pain to them, or any other deſcription of men. But truth is not to be ſacrificed to civility, nor duty to complaiſance. Nor ſhould the reverence or fear of any man, or any ſet of men, however numerous and powerful, deter the friends of humanity (they ſhall moſt aſſuredly never deter me, though coupled as they have been with threats of aſſaſſination) from pleading the cauſe of the miſerable and oppreſſed. If from a falſe point of delicacy and tenderneſs to the planters, the true ſtate of their ſlaves is never to be inveſtigated, or made known to the world, by thoſe who are perfectly well acquainted with it, it is impoſſible that their miſeries ſhould ever be removed or alleviated, or any improve-

having expreſſed myſelf with ſufficient ardour and indignation ; for not having been animated with the enthuſiaſm of a Rouſſeau or a Raynal on topicks ſo intereſting to humanity. See Monthly Review for June and July 1784, and June 1785.

ments

ments be made in their fituation. But this is rather too much to be given up in a compliment.

It is, at the fame time, but juftice to the flave-holders to acknowledge that the wretched condition, and much of the ill treatment of flaves, is not fo much a charge againft them, as againft flavery itfelf in general. Arbitrary, or unde-fined power of any kind, is too danger-ous an engine to be trufted in the hands of any man whatever. It ever has been, and ever will be abufed, and with as much of hurt to the tyrant, as of fuffer-ing to the flave. Human nature was not originally intended to fupport either the one, or the other character. It is the very nature of this pernicious authority, that is chiefly anfwerable for all the op-preffion and outrage to humanity that every man of feeling muft obferve and lament in the fugar colonies.

For

For the credit of the planter, therefore, as well as for the relief of the negroe; and let me add alfo, becaufe all
perfonal flavery, and ftill more trading in
flaves, though perhaps not forbidden in
direct terms, are diametrically oppofite
to the whole fpirit and temper of the
Chriftian religion; I muft once more re-
peat my wifh, that fome fafe, prudent,
and practicable method of emancipating
the negroe flaves, and employing them
afterwards as hired day labourers, might
in convenient time be adopted.

Let me not, however, be mifunder-
ftood. By emancipation, I do not mean
(what my antagonifts choofe, without
the leaft ground, to afcribe to me) a
fudden, univerfal, and *violent* abolition of
flavery throughout the world. This
would be as pernicious to the flave, as
unjuft to the mafter; nor is any propofal
like this to be found in my Effay. See
p. 127. 286. No fcheme of this nature
ought

ought to be attempted, (and this I have repeatedly faid) but with the utmoft caution, prudence, and deliberation, flowly, gradually, and almoft imperceptibly; firft, humanizing and civilizing the negroes, advancing them in fociety, inftructing them in Chriftianity, giving them one privilege after another, as they are able to bear them; and thus preparing them by degrees for the poffeffion, and *the right enjoyment* of freedom; of which in their prefent ftate of ignorance, and want of right principles of action, they would probably make a very improper ufe. This is evidently a progreffive and a beneficial plan. The accomplifhment of it is fo remote, that the prefent flave-holders cannot poffibly be affected, and certain I am their fucceffors will not be injured by it.

But all this my adverfaries ftrenuoufly contend, is *abfolutely impracticable.* It is a bold vifionary romantick chimerical project.

projeƈt. They affirm, that no free negroe
ever *did*, or ever *will*, voluntarily become
a day labourer, nor can by any tempta-
tion be induced to work as ſuch for hire.
—And this is the *ſecond* point, which,
I am told, deſerves ſome farther notice.

It is alledged, then, in the firſt place,
that the Marons, in Jamaica, and the
Charibs, in St. Vincents, are, and have
been, for a ſeries of years, to every pur-
poſe, *free negroes*, yet that none of theſe
were ever ſeen working for hire, or ever
ſhewed the leaſt diſpoſition to do ſo.

Suppoſing this to be the faƈt, it ought
to be conſidered, though theſe negroes
inhabit parts of civilized countries, yet
they are not comprehended in the laws;
police is not extended to them. They are
in a ſtate of conſtant warfare with the
civilized inhabitants; they deſpiſe their
cuſtoms, and abhor their manners. They
conneƈt the idea of ſlavery with imita-
tion;

tion; they muft therefore continue favages, while they continue diftinct. They
are juft what the Scotch Highlanders and
the Welch were before incorporation
took place, and law had extended her
influence over them. They are what the
Indian tribes in America, and what many
of the original Irifh are at this day. Now
it is well known, that none of thefe, nor
any other favages, whether *black* or *white*,
(for the colour makes no difference) ever
did, or ever will fubmit to hard labour,
as long as they can maintain themfelves
by plunder, hunting, or any other way.

But, let thefe people be completely
civilized; let them be trained from their
earlieft years in the employments of the
fields, in habits of labour; let them once
tafte of the fweets of induftry, as we
propofe for our flaves, and they will become as diligent, and as well difpofed to
work for hire as Europeans.

Indo-

Indolence is the characteriſtick of a ſavage. It is civilization alone, and early habit, that can give a turn to induſtry. No argument, therefore, can be drawn from men in a ſtate of barbarity, bred up from their infancy in idleneſs, and conſidering that freedom, which they value above all things, as connected with idleneſs, to men in an improved ſtate of ſociety, accuſtomed from their youth to hard labour, which is the ſuppoſition whereon my reaſoning is founded.

But ſetting this aſide, how could the free negroes of St. Vincent's or Jamaica find employment in the field, were they even deſirous of it? Every planter depends on his own, or the hired ſlaves of others for the culture of his grounds. If a free negroe be employed, he muſt work among ſlaves; but this a freeman would conſider as ignominious and diſgraceful; nor will he ever ſubmit to ſuch degradation, while he can maintain him-

ſelf

felf by hunting, fhooting, or fifhing. But this is not pecüliar to *negroes*; white men, in the fame circumftances, entertain exactly the fame fentiments, and have always acted precifely in the fame manner. Before favages can be civilized, they muft be fet down in a particular fpot, and be taught to draw their maintenance from the ground.

It is faid farther, that in every Weft India ifland, there are flaves, who have been made free; and of thefe, not one is ever known to have hired himfelf out to work in the fields. They all betake themfelves to lighter employments; becoming huckfters, pedlars, fifhermen, or domeftick fervants. All this is true; but for the reafon already affigned is nothing to the purpofe; for, if they work in the field they muft work with flaves; but this is a degradation to which they cannot ftoop. But if the flaves in general were gradually raifed to freedom, and if the

cuftom

cuftom were continued that they fhould work in the field for hire, the cafe would be totally altered. The numbers then freed could not find employment, but in the field labour, to which they had been accuftomed from their infancy. No doubt police ought to interpofe, and di- rect their labour to the common good; and liberal wages would make them cheerfully apply to it.

At prefent, they, who have freedom given them, are not in fufficient numbers to be under a *neceffity* of applying to field work, if it were (which it is not) *open* to them, or *creditable* for them. Nor are the wages now given to hired blacks fufficient to tempt freemen from eafier occupa- tions. Within thefe very few years, negroes wrought by the gang for 8d. per day; the common rate was 1od. and in time of the late war did not rife above 13d.¼ fterling per day. Now, if there were no difcredit in working

with

with flaves, a freeman can lay out his time to better advantage than in earning fuch wages. What wonder is it then, that a negroe fhould, under thefe circumftances, prefer an eafy employment, with good profit, to hard labour with lefs. Would not a white man do the fame? Thus far, there is no proof that averfion to labour is peculiar to *negroes*.

But we have to confider of what kind are the flaves to whom freedom is generally given in our iflands. They are either concubines, or other favourite domefticks, or elfe old, infirm, wornout field negroes, ftruck off the lift by a fham manumiffion to fave their taxes. I do not recollect a *fingle inftance* of a field negroe having been made free, till he was *paft labour*; and this is confirmed above by Capt. Smith. "The laft act of kindnefs," fays he, "fhewn to a negroe, after he "is worn out by hard work, fevere "punifhment, and ficknefs from un-

C "whole-

" wholefome food, is to give him his
" freedom, when he can fcarce crawl or
" fpeak." How is it poffible then for
fuch wretches as thefe to hire themfelves
out as day labourers? or who would
employ them?

Another fact appealed to is, that
though there are feveral thoufands of free
negroes in England, yet none of them
are ever found employed in any laborious work, either in the fields or ftreets.
The fact is not *univerfally* true; for I have
known *fome* negroes in England, and
have heard of others, who have wrought
as day labourers. But fuppofe the cafe
to be *in general*, as ftated. The reafon is
plain. Not one in an hundred of thofe
to be found in England *have ever worked
in the field, or been brought up from
childhood to hard labour.* They have been
bred up either as tradefmen, mechanicks,
fifhermen, or domefticks, and have either got privately away, or have come
over

over with their mafters, and deferted their fervice in England. Thefe, having never been accuftomed to field labour in their youth, cannot bring themfelves to it when advanced in years. And thofe few who may be able and willing to work, being acquainted with no other place but London, know not how or where to apply for country work; nor would the farmers employ them if they did apply, having labourers in abundance in their own villages, and being afraid of bringing in ftrangers, left they become burdenfome. My own opinion is, that moft of thofe, who are to be found in England, are above field labour. But, unlefs there be a charm in the expreffion *field labour*, they are not therefore incapable of being made ufeful. They particularly take eafily to a fea life, and become carpenters and caulkers, and very excellent feamen. I knew myfelf one, who had raifed himfelf to be captain of the forecaftle, in a well-manned frigate.

In

In fhort, there is not *a fingle cafe in point, a fingle fact that comes home to the queftion*, produced by the advocates for negroe flavery. No conclufion can be drawn againft the *poffibility* of cultivating the fugar cane by *free negroes*, from the general idlenefs either of the favage Charibs in St. Vincents, or of the Marons in Jamaica, or of the worn-out field flaves, or of the domefticks made free in the Weft Indies, or of the run-away black fervants in England. None of thefe are in the fituation of thofe for whom I propofe freedom. None of them are negroes who have been bred up from childhood in field work, in habits of induftry and labour, who are civilized, are made good men and good Chriftians, are allowed fome of the privileges of our common nature, enjoy fome of the comforts of focial life, and are thus prepared gradually for freedom, are then actually made free in the vigour of their health and ftrength, while their affections are lively,

lively, and all the tender ties of a family operate ſtrongly on them: who are then retained by previous ſtipulations and judicious regulations as day labourers, at a fair and equitable rate, and have their work allotted them with other freemen, not with ſlaves. Theſe are the perſons I mean, who, I ſay, will do the work of a planter better and cheaper than ſlaves. With *ſuch labourers as theſe, and in ſufficient numbers,* an experiment *has never yet been fairly and fully made*; and till it has, my opponents have no right to ſay, that *negroes diſcreetly manumitted* will not, and cannot, be made to work as day labourers.

There is, indeed, a ſhadow of freedom, which, though attended with many ill conſequences in particular inſtances, may yet ſerve to ſhew what negroes might do in a ſtate of real freedom. Maſters and miſtreſſes, not connected with plantations, allow their ſlaves to find work for

them-

themfelves, paying them a certain ftipu-lated fum. Sometimes it muft be owned, that the methods ufed to earn this fum, are fcandalous and bafe. But it is well known, that *fober induftrious flaves* will carefully pay their mafters this hire, and lay by perhaps as much more for them-felves. In all the iflands, but particu-larly in Barbadoes, there are numbers of white families almoft entirely fupport-ed by this voluntary labour of one, two, or a few flaves hiring themfelves out to work for other people. Will any man venture to affert, that fuch flaves would not *equally* exert themfelves were they made free, for their own or their families interefts? Will ftripes and chains operate more powerfully than hunger, diftinction, and that univer-fal inftinct, which we know every other creature exerts for its offspring, all taken together? It is a mockery to reafon but to pretend to doubt of this.

But

But to put this matter beyond all doubt, I have it in my power to anfwer the challenge, and produce a pofitive fact in proof of my affertion, that free negroes may be employed advantageoufly as voluntary labourers.

In Pennfylvania, the Quakers have freed their flaves. Thofe who have been manumitted have taken moftly to field labour. They make good labourers, and live reputably and well. Many of them are much attached to their old mafters. Some, who had given all their flaves their liberty, and now employ them at day wages, find their farms anfwer better and more profitably than before. They are employed in the culture of corn, maize, tobacco, and every fpecies of hufbandry.

This is fo full and pofitive an anfwer to the objection, that if all our reafoning on the fubject were gainfayed, it muft

C 4 continue

continue to filence the advocates for flavery, till it be as fully and pofitively proved falfe.

So much for the poffibility of cultivating fugar plantations with *free negroes*; I add, that if neceffary, which now it is not, it may alfo be done by *white labourers*.

It is a little fingular, and founds fomething like a contradiction, that the very fame gentlemen who affirm that free negroes are not fit for working in the field as hired labourers, maintain alfo, that negroes are *the only people capable of field work* in a Weft Indian climate; and that white men are not equal to the labour of a fugar plantation. But this pofition is as falfe and groundlefs as the other. The negroe is not endued with any powers for enduring heat, but what *habit* would in time impart to a Tartar or Lapland tribe, if fettled between the tropicks. In fact, ever fince the firft fet-

tlement

tlement of the fugar colonies, *white people* have been accuftomed there to *much
harder labour* than the common plantation work. Barbadoes and the Leeward
Iflands muft indeed have been originally
cleared from wood by the labour of *white
men*; and the clearing of land from wood
is *beyond all comparifon harder* than the
ordinary field work in a fugar plantation.
When the iflands of Nevis and St. Kitt's,
about 130 years ago, contained a militia
of upwards of 15000 men, and of courfe
muft, at a very low calculation, have
contained upwards of 50000 inhabitants;
could they and their families have fub-
fifted by the labour of flaves alone? The
fact is, the flave trade was then in its infancy, and the few negroes that were
introduced were rather fellow labourers
than flaves.

In England, workmen in glafs houfes,
and fmiths in forging fhip anchors,
work in á much more violent and ener-
vating

vating heat, than that of the fun between the tropicks. In the Weft Indies, the trades of blackfmith, houfe carpenter, mafon, and fhipwright, the loading and unloading of fugar fhips, are all performed by white men, who, when they are fober and careful of themfelves, do not materially fuffer by it. Yet all thefe employments are more laborious there than tilling of the ground. Plantation work is not, indeed, in itfelf hard. It is the ufe of *ftrength* inftead of *contrivance*; it is the want of food, clothes, reft, and fleep, that wears flaves out. It is the drawling out their tafk from early dawn to dufky night; it is the wandering three or four miles under the meridian fun to pick up their bundles of grafs, that conftitute their hardfhips.

If they were properly clothed and fed; if the hours of labour were judicioufly allotted; if a little more method were employed in affigning their tafks, much

more

more work might be done than at prefent, without impairing their ftrength,
or hurting their health. And, under thefe
regulations, the fame work might be
done by *white men*, if they would but
refolve to be fober, and abftain from the
exceffive ufe of rum, to which they generally fall victims. In fact, if there be
any difference between black and white
labourers, it is to be wholly afcribed to
the fuperior degree of fobriety and regu-
larity to be found among the blacks.*

* For this, alfo, we have a competent eye-witnefs in
Mr. Wefley, he fays, p. 20, of his Thoughts on Slavery,
" White men, even Englifhmen, are well able to labour
" in hot climates, provided they are temperate both in
" meat and drink, and that they inure themfelves to it
" by degrees. I fpeak no more than I know by ex-
" perience. I and my family, eight in number, em-
" ployed all our fpare time, while in Georgia," (a
climate hotter, and ten times more unfavourable to the
human conftitution than the Weft Indian iflands) " in
" felling of trees, and clearing of ground; as hard
" labour as any negroe need be employed in. The
" German family, likewife, forty in number, were em-
" ployed in all manner of labour. And this was fo far
" from impairing our health, that we all continued per-
" fectly well, while the idle ones, round about us,
" were fwept away as with a peftilence."

The

The negroes, now, in our colonies, if properly treated, and their work judiciouſly allotted, are ſufficient for the culture of all our preſent colonies; but if they were not ſo, there is no natural inability to make white labourers inadequate to the taſk. And, on the whole, we are warranted for concluding, that the work might be done to advantage by *free labourers,* whether black or white. Nay, I have the celebrated Dean of Glouceſter on my ſide, affirming that freemen might cultivate them to much more advantage, and of conſequence that ſugars might be much cheaper than they are at preſent. Of this he remarks one ſtriking proof: '' In the Britiſh iſlands,'' ſays he, '' the common price of ſugars, in time '' of peace, is generally found to be about '' 25s. ſterling per cwt. In the Eaſt In- '' dies, as I am credibly informed, it is '' no more than 2s. 6d. And what is the '' reaſon of this? Why, in the Weſt In- '' dies the ſugar is raiſed and manufac- '' tured by *ſlaves;* in the Eaſt Indies by '' *free-*

" *freemen only.*" See Difpute between Great Britain and Ireland, p. 13. See alfo my Effay, p. 116.

But after all that has been faid on this point, I wifh to have it *clearly and diftinct-ly underftood,* that though all my reafonings refpecting the *gradual emancipation* of the negroes, and the practicability of employing them or others as free labourers, fhould prove lefs folid than many perfons of the foundeft judgment think them to be; yet this would not in the leaft affect *the great and principal object* of my Effay. Though I fincerely hope, that *fome* plan will be devifed for the future gradual abolition of flavery; and though I am convinced that this may, without any prejudice to the planter, or injury to commerce, be brought about by fome fuch progreffive method as is pointed out in the Effay; yet this was not the firft, or immediate object of that book. What I had chiefly in view there, was to prove and eftablifh thefe two points.

1ft.

1ft. That the negroe flaves in the British Weft India iflands are in general (though with feveral exceptions) ill clothed, ill fed, too hardly worked, and too feverely punifhed.

2d. That matters of this importance to good government and humanity, ought no longer to be left to the difcretion of mafters and the caprice of overfeers; but fhould be regulated by fixed and written laws: that the flaves fhould be inftructed thoroughly in the principles, and trained up in the practice, of morality and religion; fhould be confidered as men, and treated as rational beings, intitled to the benefits of focial life, and indulged with more of its comforts than they now poffefs. See Effay, p. 281, &c.

The firft of thefe propofitions, I have proved by the beft evidence of which the fubject is capable; by the production of facts, to which I myfelf was a witnefs

for

for near twenty years, and by the additional teftimony of a gentleman of unqueftionable veracity, as given in the preceding letter: to which may be added, that of all the writers above mentiòned, (feveral of them men of diftinguifhed charaǎers) who all, without any previous communication, unanimoufly agree in the fame opinion; if it were neceffary, I might add my antagonift's conceffions as noted in my Reply.

The confequence muft be, that the neceffity of carrying into execution the improvements fpecified in the fecond propofition is evident and incontrovertible. My adverfaries themfelves allow this neceffity. They exprefs in very ftrong terms their approbation of that fection of the Effay, which recommends fuch improvements; and, in doing this, they approve what I confider as *the moft effential and important part of the whole book*; which will gradually, and in time, perfeǎ my every wifh on the fubjeǎ.

If

If, therefore, thefe gentlemen are fin-
cere (and why fhould we doubt them)
in the wifh they exprefs, (Curfory Re-
mark, p. 4.) *that the bleffings of freedom
may in due time be extended over the face
of the whole globe*, and of courfe to *the
negroe flaves*, among others; if they will
be fo far confiftent, as to give a fair hear-
ing, and a fair trial, to the propofals
made by others for accomplifhing this,
their own benevolent wifh, for what I
dare to add will be their own profit; or
will themfelves propofe fomething better; and in the mean time will, to the
utmoft of their power, encourage and
promote the extenfion of thofe privileges
and benefits to the negroe flaves, which
are fuggefted by me, and approved by
them, we fhall hereafter have no difference, becaufe it will appear that we
mean precifely the fame thing.

JAMES RAMSAY.

Tefton,
Feb. 20, 1786.

POSTSCRIPT.

SINCE the above went to the prefs, a fourth anonymous Apology for Slavery has made its appearance. It contains no femblance of argument that is new, or that has not been already anfwered. Its charges againft me of fanaticifm, cruelty, drunkennefs, motives of queftionable fhape, of having lately publifhed a Rhapfody, (which is not yet in print) while the accufer conceals his name, and fets out with acknowledging, " he knows neither my perfon nor cha- " racter," I fhall leave to the Reader's candour, as unworthy of any particular contradiction.

I rather wifh to call the publick attention to the Prefent State of our African Slave Trade. The French are fo intent on the improvement of Hifpaniola, and their planters, by chiefly refiding

on

on their plantations, are fo well able to
give high prices for flaves, that they
have drawn a great proportion of the
flave trade to that colony; the average
price of flaves being there from 45l. to
47l. fterling per head, while in other
colonies they cannot afford to give
above 35l.

Yet, notwithftanding thefe high prices,
fuch at prefent are the difficulties of
procuring flaves on the coaft of Africa,
that the trade is not near fo profitable as
formerly; fhips being fitted out for the
flave trade rather to oblige particular
captains than with a view to any con-
fiderable gain. Here then are we en-
gaged in a fcandalous and not very ad-
vantageous commerce, to improve the
French fugar colonies. For though it
be very poffible that the French planter
may, by giving fuch high prices, lofe
in extending his plantation, yet, every
new acre of land put in fugar canes is an
addition

addition to the publick ſtock; it employs additional ſailors, and additional ſhipping, and thus extends the nurſery of a rival navy. What motives of prudence, added to thoſe of humanity, for a thorough parliamentary inveſtigation of this horrid trade!

F I N I S.

Books Printed and Sold by J. PHILLIPS.

ESSAY on the TREATMENT and CONVERSION of AFRICAN SLAVES in the BRITISH Sugar Colonies. By the Rev. J. RAMSAY, Vicar of Tefton in Kent, who refided many Years in the West-Indies. In One Volume, Octavo. Price 5s bound, or 4s in Boards.

An INQUIRY into the Effects of putting a Stop to the African Slave Trade, and of granting Liberty to the Slaves in the Britifh Sugar Colonies. By J. RAMSAY. Price 6d.

A REPLY to the Perfonal Invectives and Objections contained in two Anfwers, publifhed by certain anonymous Perfons, to an Effay on the Treatment and Converfion of African Slaves, in the Britifh Colonies. By JAMES RAMSAY. Price 2s.

THOUGHTS on the Slavery of the Negroes. Price 4d.

The CASE of our Fellow-Creatures, the Oppreffed Africans, refpectfully recommended to the ferious Confideration of the Legiflature of Great-Britain, by the People called Quakers. Price 2d.

A SERIOUS ADDRESS to the Rulers of America, on the Inconfiftency of their Conduct refpecting Slavery. Price 3d.

A CAUTION to GREAT BRITAIN and her Colonies, in a fhort Reprefentation of the calamitous State of the enflaved Negroes in the Britifh Dominions. By ANTHONY BENEZET. Price 6d.

A Defcription of Guinea, its Situation, Produce, and the general Difpofition of its Inhabitants; with an Inquiry into the Rife and Progrefs of the Slave Trade, &c. By ANTHONY BENEZET. Bound 2s. 6d.

G# 50645041G

www.ingramcontent.com/pod-product-compliance
Lightning Source LLC
Chambersburg PA
CBHW031746090426
42739CB00008B/900